Knowing Wholeness
Through Poetry and Imagery

Nancy S.B. Ging

BALBOA.
PRESS

A DIVISION OF HAY HOUSE

Balboa Press books may be ordered through booksellers or by contacting:

Balboa Press
A Division of Hay House
1663 Liberty Drive
Bloomington, IN 47403
www.balboapress.com
1 (877) 407-4847

Because of the dynamic nature of the Internet, any web addresses or links contained in this book may have changed since publication and may no longer be valid. The views expressed in this work are solely those of the author and do not necessarily reflect the views of the publisher, and the publisher hereby disclaims any responsibility for them.

The author of this book does not dispense medical advice or prescribe the use of any technique as a form of treatment for physical, emotional, or medical problems without the advice of a physician, either directly or indirectly. The intent of the author is only to offer information of a general nature to help you in your quest for emotional and spiritual well-being. In the event you use any of the information in this book for yourself, which is your constitutional right, the author and the publisher assume no responsibility for your actions.

Print information available on the last page.

ISBN: 978-1-5043-6048-7 (sc)
ISBN: 978-1-5043-6066-1 (e)

Library of Congress Control Number: 2016909984

Balboa Press rev. date: 07/07/2016

Author's Previous Publications

Simplifying the Road to Wholeness
Published by Xlibris (2001)

Monthly Columnist 2004-2009
"Whole Brain Advisor"
Published by Conscious Choice magazine
See Archive of Articles, www.nancyging.com

"Sister/Brother Can you Paradigm?", Society for Spirituality
and Social Work Forum, Spring 1997, Vol. 4., No. 1, pg 9.

"Body Bliss", Meditation issue of Evolving
Your Spirit Magazine, May 2008.

Book review of Anne Lamott's, *Traveling Mercies*, In Her Own
Voice, a publication of INNANA, Vol.7, No.1, Summer 2001.

Book Review of *Healing Words* by Larry Dossey, M.D.
Published in the Journal of Supervision and Training in Ministry
Vol. 16, 1995

Acknowledgement

With heartfelt gratitude to my amazing assistant, Christine Romy. Without her invaluable help this book would not have come to fruition.

Dedications

This book is dedicated to L. Robin Condro, L.C.S.W.,
my brilliant shamanic healer

and

To the memory of Philip Straton Stamatakos
July 14, 1963 - April 15, 2016

CONTENTS

Preamble Ramblings

The poetry herein was written for the purpose of moving energy, my own energy. Stuck energy has too often robbed me of my aliveness. Days and months adding up to years of depression have been costly to me. Sometimes angst about romance gone awry, as described in the section, "On Loving and Leaving Narcissists", created stagnant energy which needed to be moved. Energy blockages, contracted energies need to be chased out of our energy field. Some of the poems herein suggest how that might be done.

Many of the poems were written in celebration of joy, aliveness – energy which was not contracted or stuck but fully expanded. Heartfelt joy that wanted to be expressed but not necessarily shared.

No one but the author was meant to see these, originally. Many of the poems were written in between 1998 and 2001. I had not planned to publish them but I've been encouraged to do so by those who responded to the few poems that were included in my first book, *Simplifying The Road to Wholeness*, a practical self-help book and also a friendly text book. It is full of teachings for counselors wanting to include wholesome spirituality in their practice. That first book, for me, was about integrating what I call "The Energy Paradigm" within the limited reality on which conventional Western science is based. (See appendixes i and ii in this book).

Some of the alleged poems herein are merely ramblings, notes about the ups and downs of my life. Perhaps I've had too much of the human condition about which to ramble, muse or mumble. Yet the joy and Light which has been present frequently, especially in my work with clients, has been substantial.

Many of the poems herein tell of heartfelt wholeness, only to have lost it, lost touch with the reality of wholeness, ultimate reality. Stagnation, stuck energy showed up again. Perhaps the title of this book should be Wholeness Found, Then Forgotten, Then Found Again. My next collection of poems may be called Remembering Wholeness as in my 70th decade, having been diagnosed with a life threatening medical condition in 2007 and a little breast cancer in 2011, it is easier to remember more consistently who I am, who we all truly are at heart...... and Soul.

There is a poet within each of us. Exercise yours!

Nancy Ging, 2016

Section I

ONENESS

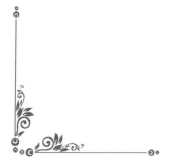

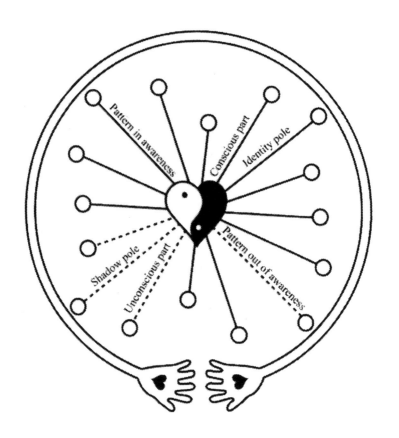

Oh, spacious soul,
My grand container
Which heals and holds this life's sum total,
You nurture possibilities within --
As waves you flow
Beyond the fleshy boundaries of my skin.
You fold within your arms my personality,
You hold and yet you set me free
For as I'm conscious of your energy
I AM expanded, grandly
Connecting, then, with One and All
And listening, I hear "the call."

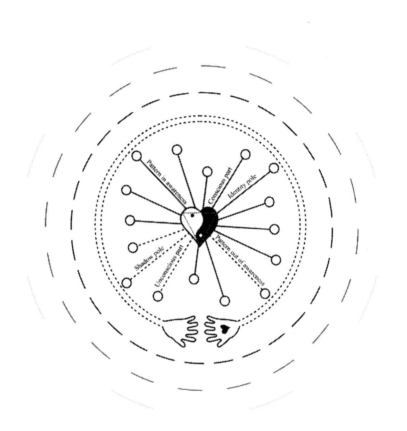

Pattern in awareness

Conscious part

Identity pole

Shadow pole

Unconscious part

Pattern out of awareness

Our Soul contains our humanness
Embraces each securely.
While holding us together as a being,
Holding us in love,
It also flows forth
Far it goes
Then farther on beyond
Until it merges with the All
Where we are surely One.

*I*t's been said
That in God's image we've been made;
If God is "All That Is,"
It's surely true
That "All That Is" wants for me, for you
All that is possible.

The following poem was set to music by Kevin Reger. He sang and recorded it at an A.R.E. (Edgar Cayce foundation) Conference in Whitewater, WI, April, 2011. Nancy Ging wrote the lyrics in 1999 after a high spirited day at an Akashic Records training group. That day in "the record" brought to an end a painful six-week period of stuck energy for me, and I moved back into my wholeness, my soul, my truth. It inspired this sing-song-like poem:

If only we remembered
How GOOD God is,
How Holy is the Whole, the "All That Is."
If only we remembered how we're loved
By Spirit, "All That Is," in Heaven above,
Heaven within, around and through
Heaven in me, Heaven in you;
The joy within our soul
Is clearly a reflection of the Whole;
The "All That Is" holds dark and light;
How is it that the total is so bright?
If only we remembered that bright spark,
The joy that Heaven holds, when all is dark;
We're not at all alone, we're always loved
The Whole holds us, we're known above;
We're fed, we're nurtured, calmed by Earth below
This Mother Planet Earth her gifts bestows;
All we need is here for us to claim;
She wants us to RECEIVE.
                    Release the pain!
If only we remembered in our drought
The resource, love and joy that's all about.

Section 2

DUALITY AND DIVERSITY; THE ONE AND THE MANY PAIRS OF OPPOSITES

Noah's Ark may be the heart,
The grand container
Of the Soul which holds, enfolds
The pairs of energies, opposite parts.

See Appendix i for detailed story, a new take on Noah.

Diversity, a certainty
Equal we can't be
> In terms of energy
> Nor talent, beauty;
But equally we share
> A Soulful goal,
> Our choice to serve collectively,
> Perhaps a duty,
> Which is: to know our wholeness.
This is ALL we're here for.
We are here for ALL,
Our wholeness, knowing of it
Tells us our totality,
Shows us equally the holy, All That Is.
That is all;
Within ourselves
> As it is so
> Without --
> That is, within the great Beyond.
> As above, so below.
Simply, this is it ---
To know,
> Then go
> Enjoy
> It All.

I pray
Let us be friends
Put peace on Earth together
You are my long lost sisters
You are my precious brothers
We have one mother, Earth
We share the same Creator
These parents meant this human family
To live enjoying harmony
Within our hearts we share this truth
Our clothes, our skin, our customs
Show diversity
Yet our human family
Each member of humanity
Shares a similarity
A heart within a breast that knows
That this is so
Both Mother Earth and Father Sun
Want us to co-create
The peace
And carry out what was begun
In joy
An end to war
now sweet relief.

When so divergent,
Far from friendly
Are a pair of energies within,
See an image
In your mind's eye
Put them on a see-saw
Gazing in the other's eyes
Exchanging just a bit
                or more
Of the other's vibes
Energetic empathy comes forth
Polarities can now find peace.
This works with parts within
It's true for people, too.
Choose
To be amused
Play with energy.

$\mathscr{P}$olarities Sharing a See-Saw

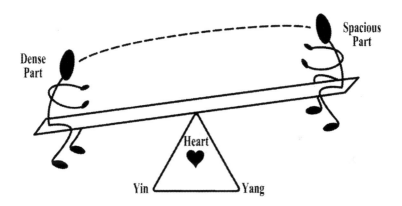

Section 3

BE THE TRINITY

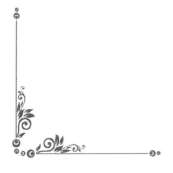

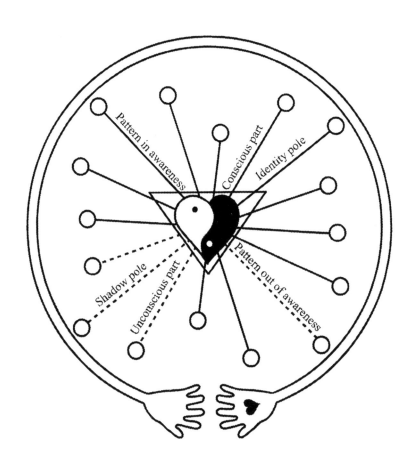

Two hemispheres and one heart
Meet to make a trinity for living;
Two perspectives of reality from mind
May find their greatest advocate in giving
Sovereignty to a heart awakened.
Once this heart-brain triangle we know
Lives will link with Grace, toward calling's flow.
As we activate and honor this grand trine
Lives become more humane, more Divine.

Triangles
The angles/angels
Numbers of these letters
Sharing such vibrations
Sacred shapes
And circles like our Souls
Honoring Geometry

A trinity of flames
A trio of flickering lights
Picture such a candle flame at
    low abdomen initially
    then see a flame within the heart
    and finally at the forehead
Watch for the hue of violet
Saint Germain may come to you
Allow that three-fold flame
To slowly, surely
Burn together as ONE
Alight your soul

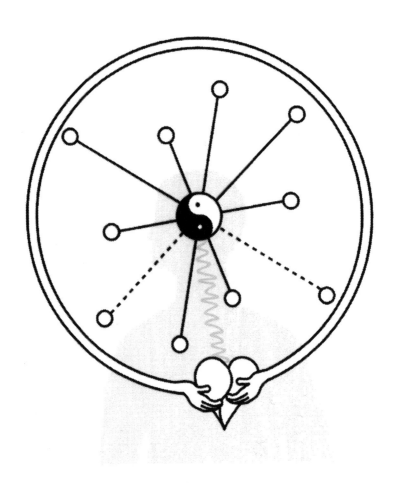

Meet me in the middle,
Go to heart below.
A brain's tense desperation
Finds solace in the glow
Above the belly's urges,
And loins which long to mate
The heart's the only haven,
Where forces compensate.

*h*ead, heart and hara
the heart's the place to start
begin within the sacred soul
held in the breast
the best beginning
acclimating to the energies divine
whatever time it takes
be with the love that has no need
and then forgetting speed
you slide below
go slow
so slowly moving through
the torso blocked with fear and greed,
taking heart's unique vibrations with you
 as you go
move on through
to find a candle flame aglow
within the womb-like space of power
so named your Dan Tien, your Hara,
bring grace upon that place
and going down
in time to ground
move through your root or tail bone's tip
enjoy the trip to Mother's Center
Earth below
where once there you give a gift to her:
your woes, your aches and foes
your human heart delivers to The Mother
all your human needs, concerns for little self and other.

Section 4

QUADRANTS OF THE HEART

Four compartments has the heart,
Housing all its qualities;
Two Yin, two Yang chambers apart
Meet Soul at their interstices

Stout hearted, tender hearted,
Heart both Yang and Yin
Four chambered gem you are
Soul is found within

Come kindness,
softness,
gentle flowing ripples
of a heart's vibration;
replace the harshness
of the mind's calculations,
cold with judgement,
and evaluation;
come instead with kindness,
soft as baby's blanket
now's the time
and here's the place
for grace and loving kindness;
do descend on me,
impart the peace
your ever warm and tender love can bring
and share again the wealth of your
wellspring.

Light Hearted Poems for
Heart, Head, & Hara Wholeness,

Sweet simplicity
It's bliss,
Only the heart can know this,
For bliss is not the province of the brain
Wherein, indeed, complexity does reign.
Come quiet revolution,
Internal evolution
Come heart-head marriage.
I welcome now this union
A holy whole communion
My body is the carriage.

xoxoxoxoxoxoxoxoxoxoxoxoxooxox

My heart is out to catch me!
Sweet relief it is to know
There is within me much to trust,
Not head but Soul aglow.

xoxoxoxoxoxoxoxoxoxoxoxoxoxoxox

There is a pool of joy out there;
And so it's here within, I know it well;
When you will find it, too,
Your heart and time will tell.

xoxoxoxoxoxoxoxoxoxoxoxoxoxoxoxox

Clarify my confusion, heart
As only you can do ---
Calm the creases of my cortex
And make me new.

For God, A Redwood Tree, and a New Dance:

Great One, my All,
Make me majestic as this tree
                              so tall
Through my heart's way set me free
Ignite its spark anew
And fan the fire, awaken me.
Flow forth this love
          To others
Setting free another and another,
          my heart's desire, on fire,
Until one day
          Our human family may
In joy, enjoy,
          The Old Lub Dub Dance
          Together, forever.

"**H**ope springs eternal
in the human breast."
How is it that it's taken me so long
To truly go from mind
to a place more rich, within this chest,
To make connection with the space Divine
where warmth, illumination shines,
where mental knowing is enobled with a glow
from heart's pure gold --- the love we show
when, with our attention there,
we flow into our heartspace sacred,
sharing feelings of an energy refined
beyond all manner of our thoughts ---
thoughts, though they be useful,
are not the spaces
where Grace can find it's places to reveal
the greatest of our qualities,
where sacred joins our human nature,
where bodymind meets soul
and finally, fully, we are whole.

"Hope springs Eternal...."
Words of Alexander Pope

green energy
if it is true
that this may be
the heart's own hue,
the vibratory flow,
the tone of sacred heartspace,
grace within the cavern of the chest,
then it's not surprising that the verdant blanket
Springtime brings
will also bring the heart to singing,
looking for another
one to love
with whom to share the beauty of this Earth
as everywhere
the birth of grass, of leaves on trees,
on branches holding glowing greenery
is seen and even heard
as we awaken more to consciousness
with honoring of senses secondarily
soon we will taste the colors
hear the smells, touch the sounds
and know the energy surrounding all we see,
this marriage --- consciousness and all
the bodily held senses
starting always with the heart as haven,
place to know as central
when we start adventuring
into the world's rich energies
and find that these vibrations green
will represent a heart serene

GOOD GREED AND GRATITUDE
A Thanksgiving Poem

A time for giving thanks
    This season offers me
The chance to simply notice,
    Now, a heart so full.
Great gratitude abounds
    For friends, a family
And acquaintances as well
    Who seek, as I seek,
    The expansion of awareness,
    Unfolding of full Consciousness,
The joy in knowing
    From the heart
Only All That Is
    And All That Is, is good.
In this time of thanking, blessing
    What is good,
Let us commit to live
    At ALL times from
    An attitude of gratitude
    For the Reality
    Of All That's So.
Let us, as well, embody greed
    for God,
And as we hunger and thirst
    After right-relatedness
    Within ourselves and so, within our world,
    It will be given.

Why would one
Entertain another attitude but gratitude
It holds me in the heart,
That chamber cozy, clean
So welcoming
The glow
We know there is a fireplace
     Christmas stockings
     Hanging by its' side
     Awaiting gifts, surprises
     For our inner children
This heart, this haven
This home of gratitude
How can I thank you
     Only often and always
Nothing feels so grand as this.

Written at Warrior-Monk 8-Day retreat, May 1999.

Some Poems for St. Valentine's Day

The hatching of the heart ---
So ripe, this phrase is haunting me.
How good, indeed, it would be for the world
If each of us would HATCH our HEARTS this year,
Allowing hardened shells surrounding these
To slowly crack and fall away,
Releasing Light and love with wings
So all with the orbit of our field
Could feel the flow
And somehow know
That love of every kind
Comes from the heart, not mind.
There is a circle here:
The mind informs the heart,
The heart illumes the mind
Which then, again, informs the heart ---
And so it goes; with Grace the process flows.
Celebrate anew, each day, your best of parts:
Your tender and courageous heart
And start to HATCH that HEART today;
Tomorrow, someday, set it free
Then feel your Essence, fully BE.

The phrase, "The hatching of the heart" I heard from theologian Marcus Borg during a guest sermon at Union Church, my progressive U.C.C. Church in Hinsdale, Illinois. He shared that he learned the phrase from Alan Jones.

Celebrate this day your best of parts,
The chakra of your treasured heart --
Haven for the spark of fire, a gentle might.
Here we may tenderly enfold and seal
All we've shared with warmth and Light
Let spaciousness prevail as we expand
the energy held there.
Our hearts hold all we know that's real;
Move your mind into your heart this day
And have it stay.

Lyrics for a song yet to be composed:

Our heart's the greatest treasure trove
The body-mind may hold
Compassion is its healing balm
For others to enfold.

And we as well receive this love
As often as we give it.
Benevolence is who we ARE
Remember, then, to live it.

And NOW's the time, the only place
From whence the heart can flow;
Eternity's the here and now —
The heartspace whole, a'glow.

Let's honor now the organ —
Four chambered, splendid thing,
The meeting place of Mother Earth
With Heaven's beckoning.

So clear away the discontent
And set your ticker free!
Celebrate your choice to love –
Embrace humanity!

Section 5

THE WAYS OF ENERGY

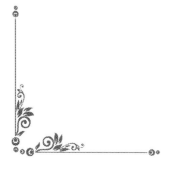

You see,
We live in more than one reality.
    We've been shown a world that's dense
    Made of objects, separate parts,
    Things, like nouns, contained within
        The very boundaries of their skin
    Or limits of another kind,
    Edges making particles distinct.
    This realm we know so well
    within the culture of the West,
    The male's "left-brain" or Yang approach
    May interpret it the best.
    Newton's physics teaches well;
        It sells us a reality of separateness,
        Differentiate
        Individuated objects,
        Parts or particles, and molecules
        Yet tells us nothing of the whole.
    There is another science for ALL this:
        Our souls relate with bliss akin to Oneness
    As Quantum Physics brings us a Reality so Holy
    Showing us that in this world there is
    nothing solely separate;
        All is One in Quantum's world;
        'Tis a world of energies which mingle

There are no distinctly separate parts
    None are alone, none are single,
But all are waves,
    Like ripples, intersecting;
In THIS realm,
    ALL is connecting --
Waves of energy, lively, dancing
So alive is life, the Chi advancing,
And evolving, ever onward, never ending.
Yet not the same is so within the solid realm.
We see that bodies die;
For those who lose a loved one to his death
Will surely feel the loss was real
    Yet energy remains, somehow.
    We speak of Spirit, Soul, forever and Eternity.
    Yin, the feminine's "right-brain" glows,
        It knows this fine Reality so well;
Sensing, dreaming, loving, trancing
Not of logic is this way,
Nothing here to solve or figure out;
Here, AWARENESS is the key,
To BE
And to begin to see the MYSTERY
To live in it, at any rate;
In this vast realm we do not problem solve
                    but we PARTICIPATE !
"Right-brain" Quantum world is, you see
That spacious, Light Reality,
That realm where ALL is One;
Of vibrations, energies here we sing;

As Buddhist to the hot dog vender:
"Make me one with everything."
All connected as with heart
Clearly, heart's the place to start
    To know about the Whole,
    The symphony of waves
Like sound vibrations, colors, smells
Giving off their energies, mingling into ours
    Love is of this realm;
The metaphor of wind's another way
    (as it's effect's we see)
    To comprehend WAVE Reality
Wind and quantum's waves
    are not the things we see,
    Although, we know their power.
    Vibrations, even of the flowers
    Give us much besides their beauty;
Finally we are learning of the ways of energy.
But let us not negate old Newton's world.
Our mind, at least, our "left-brain" knows of objects.
There, in my mind at least, exists a world of THINGS.
    An architect of Quantum Physics,
    David Bohm implied,
No nouns exist, but only sluggish verbs,
For all is PROCESS
    in the Quantum way of being led.
I know, that both these sciences are so,
Within the living of our lives,
As we experience being human, and divinely so.
To have a body here on Earth

We feel our density
And cannot always see
Our life as Quantum's WAVE Reality.
For just as real as girl and boy are different,
So it is with life WITHIN our bodies,
Separate, dense, they seem to be ---
And yet we're also energy
Intermingling.
It may now seem confusing
To consider living in two worlds
  Not choosing one instead of other
  And yet we all are living in two homes,
Yet not so simply do we live
Without a framework of these two perspectives
And how we move so fluidly between them.
To bridge these paradigms
Has been the goal within my soul,
A theme, this dream for decades
More clearly it is coming for me now,
As I have learned to live my life, I make this vow
Within this body dense
Where Soul has taken up its residence.
To practice being present is the key
To learn to live a life that balances realities.
To separate what's meant to be a partnership
Makes us broken, lost in "sin."
A formula for living life may start
With rules : YOU MUST BE PRESENT TO WIN !
  Then dance and balance two realities,
  And partner personal polarities,

Gain awareness of a trinity of male
And female minds with heart!
Yet more than presence is required in this life;
We also must take action.
Again, again, the key
For you,
For me,
To EXPERIENCE our dense body matter and to DO
And also be AWARE, which is to BE.

January 1999

Section 6

OF LIFE'S COMPLEXITIES

Sometimes
the people who would treat us wrongfully
Are truly good,
Intending just as we are
To live a life that's just,
A life that serves the Light.
We must, then, make allowances for those
who seem to harm us
Yet they make us strong;
Feeling, such, our pain
Awaken us to claim
      The power
      Of which our souls are made;
And on we travel, travel on;
Our fate unfolds, our lives unravel
As we live consciously,
           evolve.
This Mystery we shall not solve.

Martyrdom
Is not the mode
that we must follow
anymore;
Not willingly,
at any rate.
Awaken now
before it is too late
to see that you
must BE that motto --
TO SERVE AND TO PROTECT
yourself.
Letting others drain you
Is not the way to flow.
Think energy; you'll know.
Give not your souls away;
Your kindness and your play
you share with others
gladly;
Share your love, your Light
 quite consciously
But let not others TAKE it.
Rape takes many forms.
At times there is collusion;

Always it is wrong
to take another's anything
without consent
or recompense.
Bodies, Light, ideas,
we share these joyfully;
Yet some will take
against our will
And if we value not ourselves enough,
we will participate in this
misuse of energies
of many kinds
and qualities.
Father forgive and light our minds
As we know not what we do
at times

We help
from different places
a variety of spaces
deep inside ourselves
with motives many
mixed
some innocent
and pure
some convoluted
coming from a need for drama
a distraction from our pain
by falling into traumas of another
to lift the focus from our own malaise
motives shift from stages
phases of our lives
so often gratitude inspires our actions
a desire for giving back the good
repaying the Divine for intervention
when at times we've been dejected
disconnected
rescued, resurrected
by a friend, a mentor
then again we've found our center
sometimes by helping others
we are seeking
quite unconsciously
to balance
those bad places
deep and dark within

yet always there's a spark
of Light involved
with any kind of service
lifting pain of friend or foe
lifts us as in those moments
we take on an angel glowing fragrance
as agents of the God we're born to be
whatever human else goes on
with you and me.

Denial

I loathe the liar that you are,
Distorting, bending Truth
Is unacceptable.
Yet, without your style
Of dealing with reality
How would we handle shock,
Unspeakable surprises
Much too harsh for any nervous system?
You are a necessary evil.
Not ONLY dark, dishonest
You are a necessary good
Defense as well;
You get us through
This life.
We do
Need you
At times,
Denial.

This woman's balance has been hard won;
Enormous work at growing has been done.
It's never finished, more's to come.
Just how another's life is going
Ends up showing much
About the process
And the ways of living life mysterious;
And in the hearing of these truths
We may create less strife,
Less serious pain within our own.
We gain from tales of other's lives;
We learn from stories
Of another's life that flowed
From seeds of energy they've sown
Which show the power of our hearts,
Our thoughts, our kinds of minds,
Both human and divine.
At the place these paradigms will meet
We see the making of a life complete.

*T*oday I balance two desires:
Desire to simply live a better life
     Improving habits, watching thoughts,
And a desire to realize that I HAVE REALIZED
My wholeness quite completely
For I am already whole,
Have always been complete and didn't know it.
I am already loved by my Creator
And with that force I shall align myself
Making now and then adjustments to my
     Rendition of this lifetime
What a burden can this,
my human condition be.
But lighter is it when I walk with Thee.

Section 7

LAMENTATIONS ON CONSCIOUS LOVING; CHALLENGES AND JOYS

No longer will I put myself beneath
>Another
>Lover
>Or any other -- anyone.
For here and now
I speak about my worth.
Equal we are not
>In terms of energy
>Or talent, beauty;
But equally we share
>Our only work of life, our task,
>Which is: to know our wholeness.
This is ALL that we are here for.
We are here for ALL,
Our wholeness, knowing of it
Tells us our totality,
Shows us equally the holy, All That Is.
That is all;
Within ourselves
>As it is so
>Without
>That is, within the great Beyond.
Simply, this is it
To know,
>Then go
>Enjoy
>It All.

There is nothing to lose in loving you
Nothing to lose
Great is the cost
in ignoring the rules
risking so foolishly
pain for no gain
this alliance can bring
at this time, in this Spring
Yet from afar
And close as the soul of me
I find voluminous peace and love
In the whole of me
when I recall
Who truly you are
And who you can be

You were a gift.
You lifted me to Light I hadn't known before
And more there was in store for me
If only I had rightly seen the brightness of it sooner.
Why don't I listen when I get "the call" from God?
But I have learned to listen, now:
"Surrender, dear," God says to me.
"Surrender deeply,
more than ever you have done before.
The gift which lifted you,
you turned away from with your mind.
You closed your heart,
let patterns of the past then bind you.
Bless you for your willingness to see
These painful new awareness's, reality.
Now grieve, dear girl, for your beloved Ricky."

Who was he, Mister B. ?
Only the kindest one,
The best I ever knew.
Only the warmest.
So sensitive was he.
So sensitive a soul.
He looked me in the eyes with
Willingness to meet
In Soul to Soul communication.
He told the truth most often.
I trusted him with everything.
For seeing truth in people,
Justice in the world,
He was a master in my eyes.
Discretion, wisdom was
The order of the day for him
Until this holocaust upon our
Holy, Whole connection.
Fair conduct was his way
In times before this misery.
For sharing of a film
No one was better.
In meditation he was pure,
Connected to the source, he was.
Committed to his role of service,
Spent his life in acts of kindness,
Wisdom, calming, soothing those in pain.
You can remember, then, his goodness.
Throw away the pain he's caused today.

Remember, focus on the gratitude
That you have known this gift at all.
Three times, the sacred trinity of times
He came into your life and loved you so.
It wasn't only his attachment needs that brought him
To me, was it?
Perhaps it was.
Perhaps I mattered very little,
For, oh, so easily he's moved along
To other places, women who may give
What I withheld in my attempt to
Do what I believed God wanted
Me to do.
So write I can't,
Not anymore.
It cost too much.
For he has trashed the friendship.
He's distorted much of what we had,
Forgotten all about the love,
Wants not to hear a thing from me.
The plan I thought the Spirit
Had in store for us is shattered.
So wrong was I to make my writing all that mattered

O.K.

I let it go today.
I let it go for good.
Something said I should.
Pray peace will come
And no harm done
To what is left.
I feel bereft
Of this dear friend.
Dear God please take it;
Let it mend and make it
Smooth again,
The rhythm of the flow.
Send Mercy here, below.
It's in your hands.
I have no plans
Except releasing sorrow
Today,
    again
      tomorrow.

Am I not much good at love?
The value
Which I've held
As most important to me,
I've sometimes failed at living out,
Failed at giving to another one significant to me.
I am learning much too late
The whys and ways I close the flow,
Shut down the damper on the fireplace of my heart.
My love is great,
My fire pure when not snuffed out.
Why must I close my heart's door to another?
John in college, Tom in marriage,
Ricky now, a golden chance at love
I've ruined.
If only he had pointed out,
"You're doing it again," he could have shouted!
"Shut NOT your heart down, Nancy love,"
He could have said,
He could have read my mind,
He could have coaxed me back to love
He could have given me a look
Reminding me to stay,
That's all it took to melt away the shell
I formed which caused this hell
Of loss and grief,
Remorse so great.
There's nothing worse
Than learning this too late.

Know, John
Though the years move on
Specific memories remain
Precisely etched, profoundly placed,
Exquisitely they're sketched and soldered
In my soul.
My heart and mind,
My body sense review,
And will remember
you.

Section 8

ON LOVING AND LEAVING NARCISSISTS

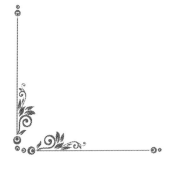

He vastly under-rated me
He never even dated me
And all seems lost
He put me in a double bind
He wasn't altogether kind
There was a cost
I wanted so to be his friend
Considered it might never end
So sad, exhausted
I hoped to bring some joy to him
My light and love is rarely dim
He's left me feeling low, accosted

What I wanted was to share
      And to connect;
To share a portion of the bounty
      That life has given me,
A portion of my love, concern,
      My energy.
A time or two I thought I saw the soul of you.
In my eagerness to help support your growth
I gave beyond the scope
Of what was wise for me to do,
Wanting much too much to share
      The learnings of my life
      Assuming these would help you, too.
And as I longed to share,
      Connect with you, in friendship,
      Wanting to support your life unfolding
There was, will always be in me,
      A need to lay, be free,
      To dance,
      To snuggle softly, happily
Sharing in the banquet which life offers
      Through our senses;
Rather than to starve to death in isolation
I choose to let that feast begin anew
      With you,
Your warmth, your sense of wonder, depth/intensity
      Attracting me to you,
Desiring tender contour contact,
      And yes, passion

Knowing joy together, many ways
    In any fashion,
My former isolation, like a prision,
Longs to be undone
    Or balanced now
With play, with joy, with sharing song and senses.
We had begun to build a friendship,
    A container safe and sensuous,
    A place for tasting of Life's pleasures,
    Of sharing comfort, words, ideas as well;
But pain befell this friendship; fear began to swell.
And so
    On we go,
    Moving now toward others
    We each proceed
    Asking Life to bring us what we need.

Shatter not my Spirit, Mister Friend.
I thought you were my friend, my pal,
A precious kindred spirit on this path to Kingdom Come,
Someone with who to share some pieces of the journey
A presence, now, with whom to tell our truths
Those truths, both yours and mine;
A friend so bright, so full of light.
Now comes this news, for which I asked,
of how you see me.
So much of what you say is wise, and true,
Perceptive,
Yet you've forgotten what has come to pass for me
        since last the moon was full.
We do not know each other, really.
With some degree of trepidation
I'll approach you from now on,
Anticipating harshness, judgement, force and might
When once I only knew the joy and light, the play
This is another day.
Heaven knows it it is safe enough
        to open wide my heart again in friendship.
I believe I will.
It may be rough; your words are tough
And I am tender.
Strong, with love, I am as well.
If I am wanting, willing to communicate with greater care,
Awareness,
Kindness,
        Would you be wanting,
                willing, seeking now to do the same?

Section 9

WRITE POETRY, MOVE ENERGY

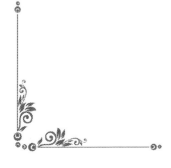

Come muse
Amuse me
once again
Send words into my pen
amending mental ways
the harsh
gymnastics of the mind
are put aside
when you my poet
come to play
you move me into daylight
dancing partner
for sublime realities
principalities divine
come muse again
you're mine
enchanted flowing
friend

A poem cannot be written from my brain
For what my heart alone can know
Must freely from the body flow
So sensual the words around me
Find their places
Filling spaces
They surround me
Giving solace as they come
Or joy, if that is of the mode
I carry in the moment.
Poetry, a friend you are
A gift to me
For healing,
Celebration too;
And you are like this poet:
One who chooses
Many moods and ways
For fully living every day;
Words, much fun with which to play,
Soul, such wealth you have to share
Gratefully, I've found you now.
More to come, for certain, more to say.

The remainder of the writing in this section are the first items I wrote at the suggestion of my massage therapist. The goal was to move myself out of pain that seemed for weeks cemented within me from a romance with yet another narcissist. Having never written poetry before, I was surprised that all the pain vanished after I expressed it through these cathartic ramblings. I share the following pieces to give the reader encouragement to spew out feelings in at least semi-poetic fashion. Peace came to me after such a catharsis.

She told me to write poetry
        to heal myself--
To mend
Post potent romance
Perhaps this pen to paper
Puts me in a place most primal
Where the longings are most pure,
        unadulterated
Pure, primary, deepest urge to be most real,
To heal
With him I wanted only to feel the love and freedom —
No dependency here, really
Only true union of hearts —
A wealth of feeling,
        the feeling of deep peace so rich —
Before he had to push away—
        and push away again –
           to be safe?
           to be cruel?
God knows one longs for union
        with one's Self
And in our meeting in the energy of God
He found himself
He felt alive
Then ran away

It's not about me
It's about you —
　　　You say
What a fool
What a fool forgets
　　　About me
　　　About you
And how our meetings healed our pasts
In the Light of NOW
And our particular
　　　And very personal-to-us experiences
　　　Of all we both are and have been
In those moments
　　　Together
in our very our particular lives

So rare a vibrational match
Now blown asunder

Because of me
You say,
You are able now
To love another
More fully
Than you knew to do
Before
We met in Grace
What you needed
To begin
To birth yourself
I gave so freely
and so fluidly
So flowing with my life
As to attract a cardboard box
With heart in hand upon it painted
Now tainted
With the hurt,
That image,
Knowing what I do
That darkness wins
With you

Trust again?
Not me,
Not you,
Not now
Not knowing
What I now know
Of the fearfulness in you.

Who are you?
Who are you really?
Which of the many faces
Which of the many voices
Do you value as most YOU?
You as central
You as core
Whom do you want to be?
Which did I reflect?
Which does she reflect"
Whom did the Creator
       Of your Soul
Have in mind
For you to co-create
       With Him
and co-create again

It feels so fine
       So holy
        Wholey
to BE as was intended
       By Divine Creation
You most loving, strong
and at once most vulnerable
most longing to be one
with one so
       Sensitive to you as I am
Love the Mystery
And you will find the friend
       Within yourself
        Yourselves
You want you
       To be free
to be at one with me
and at the same time be most you.

So afraid of loving
So afraid to die
    You are
Not knowing yet
That death
    Gives way to Life
      Anew
Far richer
    More alive with heart
      And freedom
        Than before
Only know how good God is
To bring my Light to you
To bring YOUR Light to you
      As well
To dispel the darkness
      So compelling
      As before.
Now no longer numb
    You live a life you're liking
    Better than the one before.
Give me back my heart
And I will take it back
Knowing that it
    Gave you life anew
    Now
    Never to explore again
    The mystery of what He had in mind
      For me to be
        With you

Section 10

SENSUALITY, SEX AND SOUL

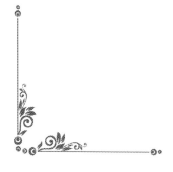

Robust
Those lusty ways
So primal
While we have these bodies
Let us get from them
The mileage that we may
Connecting to Divine aliveness
Merging with the Great Beyond
Communing with The One
Through union with another
Lover
Spirits flowing
Arms enfolding
Hearts of gold
No withholding
Share this Earth
Give birth to making
Fertile now
At any age
And any stage of life
A time for pleasure-making
No mistake in waking
To a time to savor
Bodies which have brought us through
And on beyond our suffering
To now enjoy the bonds
Of blissful union,
Sweet communion.

Below is original, less dignified version:

Robust and lusty,
Juicy, loosey--goosey
Ways so primal
Long as we have bodies
Let us get
The mileage out of them we may
With hearty bumps
With grinds
Growns/moans sublime
With ardent sighs
Connecting to divine aliveness
Humping bodies
Hurling spirits
Merging with the great beyond
Communing with The One
Through union with another
Lover
Lust enhancing
Hearts of gold
Love a'flowing
Arms enfolding
No withholding
Share this Earth
Give birth to making

Fertile now
At any age
And any stage of life
A time for pleasure-making
No mistake in waking
To a time to savor
Bodies which have brought
Us through and on beyond
Our suffering
To now enjoy the bonds
Of blissful union
Sweet communion.

For the following poem to flow,
know that Kohutian is pronounced Ka-WHO-shun.

Lusting for cohesion –
A self that I could trust
In the sense that was Kohutian –
For me it was a must.

The energy of heartfelt lust
Directed toward that goal,
Brought more than integration–
It brought me to my soul.

The poem above was shared at a professional conference on The Power of Sex -- to Hurt, to Hold, to Heal, November 14, 2003, The Family Institute, Northwestern University, Evanston, IL. My workshop was entitled, "Sex and the Unified Self" which came out of my book about the unified self, *Simplifying the Road to Wholeness* (2001).

Heinz Kohut (1913-1981) is an esteemed Psychoanalyst whose theoretical material, Self Psychology, is referred to as Kohutian. His work was an important influence on me from the mid 1970's.

At an 8-day Warrior-Monk retreat in Wisconsin in 1999
we were asked to write a poem about "Longing."

In the family of things
This one longs for making love
Not enough it is to have
    My inner male and female,
    Finally now more friendly.
I want another,
Another lover
Longing to play,
To dance more often
To share the joy of this rich Earth
To share the senses
Surely we are here to do that;
I know at least that I am.
I long as well to be
Well liberated from that
Which holds me from my calling.
I hope, I pray for more:
I long for children in this world
To be seen as holy,
Live in safety
Fed and cherished.
A time of peace must be at hand.
Surely this world is coming.

How dare you?
I am angry.
How dare you leave?
How could you
    leave this body o'mine,
Longing sorely now.
How could you
Take from me
    The ecstacy
Your loving touch
Produced in me
Such pleasure,
    So much possibility
    For sacred sex
    The future held
So powerful and good
Escape from stressful lives,
So tender, kind
This sensate sacrament
Of touching, moving me from mind,
From brain to bodyrich
You did provide for me
These feelings exquisite.
Making love the ways we did
We gave the Universe much more;
The Heavens gained a higher vibe
Whenever we would lie together,
Ride each other's sacred earth.
You've robbed me now of all of this

And on you've gone to satisfy another lover.
I practice now containing rage
By putting words upon a page
My energy now entangled in the mess
Of chaos, jangled nerves from anger.
What of my book?
Did you EVER look
At what all this would do
To what I WAS creating?
Ruined now by you, you foolish man.
In wreck and ruin lies the plan.

Section 11

STATES OF MIND

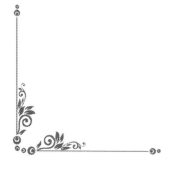

Peace is with us
    Handing us a gentle feeling:
    "Let's get on with it"
Yet sometimes
Passivity comes
Then lethargy arrives
Soon seriously stuck we be
Eventually
When we remember
We can choose --
We breathe with Consciousness
A neutral space
An energy of balance
Light and Spaciousness within
Watch the energy move on
From one mode to another
By writing poetry

We help
from different places
a variety of spaces
deep inside ourselves
with motives many
mixed
some innocent
and pure
some convoluted
coming from a need for drama
a distraction from our pain
by falling into traumas of another
to lift the focus from our own malaise
motives shift from stages
phases of our lives
so often gratitude inspires our actions
a desire for giving back the good
repaying the Divine for intervention
when at times we've been dejected
disconnected
rescued, resurrected
by a friend, a mentor
then again we've found our center
sometimes by helping others
we are seeking
quite unconsciously

to balance
those bad places
deep and dark within
yet always there's a spark
of Light involved
with any kind of service
lifting pain of friend or foe
lifts us as in those moments
we take on an angel glowing fragrance
as agents of the God we're born to be
whatever human else goes on
with you and me.

When does loving kindness
    and acceptance
Become permissiveness
Enabling destruction?
When should one say:
    "Stop!
Or reconsider;
Are you truly in alignment with the One?"
Only when those actions cause me harm
Or harm the one who acts unconsciously
Without consulting deep inside
The place where heart knows all –
Delusions do not dwell therein;
The larger picture can be found
With guidance, simplifying motivations,
Gently quieting the urges
Of our need for warmth, sensation.
The chaos calls for peace –
Surrender all, yet call for All
And move into le coeur*
Mistakes we will not make
When sovereignty of heart is sought
Yet if another seems to make them anyway
And go astray

Perhaps those actions serve the growth
For only she or he can know
The need for lessons, depth of longings
Lessons to be learned
And sharings one is urged to sow.

Written in Paris after a retreat at Taize, France

Am I
up high
upon the list:
Accomplishment
At Fearfulness Of Life?
perhaps the ninetieth percentile
is my achievement level,
such excellence in shivering,
painful living
quite immersed in fright
often feeling tightness
from the dark night of the soul
for frequently in eras past
I have inhabited
contracted forms of energy
impacting on my destiny
by slowing down reception
of abundant love connection
but year by year
this lessens
faith increases
doubt declines
diminishing returns
have been the payoff
of fearfulness
recently I've learned
that love's the gold
encoded in my heart
should I live long enough

I'll die with fear eroded
knowing lusciously and well
the safeness of the NOW
consistently and steady
fully ready then
to sweetly meet my maker
spacious good One sole
Creator

Let me have a new life!
Let me bring in joy
Without this start and stop routine:
I surge ahead with hopefulness
I flow,
Then two steps back
In retrograde I go.
Now is the time;
Stars warnings tell me so ---
Returning Saturn
Here a second time
Can bring fulfillment
And fruition of my goal
To surely know
And act upon that knowing
Of Creation's dreams for me ---
Unbridled happiness,
Abundant opportunities to share
And with my splendid love
To find, to care about a partner
Who's my equal
And all I need is to remember,
Trust and recollect the Truth
Of what is possible;
Now is the time
My age old patterns, self-defeating
Have to go.

Section 12

THE SHADOW, THAT GREMLIN

Psychiatrist Carl Jung called it the shadow -- the side of the psyche which is the opposite of our true reality – our Light. Wise are those who recognize that we all have such a dark energy in the unconscious. Owning that buried potential keeps us from acting out of it. The shadow can sabotage our dreams and goals. Its energy can be transformed into healthy power.

Oh, Saboteur
Show me what you need from me
To be transformed with dignity

Distraction reigns,
Procrastination pains me
When I forget your need,
Your greediness immense
To be remembered,
Every moment, every sentence.
Written, spoken.
Listening, now for your demands
To be included ---
I will keep you close, I will.
Ever in awareness, always
Here and now this pact I make,
Reacting to your genuine commands
And so you shall be,
From now on,
A partner, here.
Will self-defeating days be gone?
Let's paraphrase:
I AM the way, the truth and the dark/light split
And Jesus, Nazareth's
Enfante Supremo
Surely understands
That finally, I'm made whole
In our renewed duo.
Life didn't work the other way
So darkness, you are here to stay with me
In wholeness, Truth so bright;
Your darkness does not dim the Light.
The Age which is upon us here,
Says this:
When polar opposites appear
Let's welcome the dichotomies
Let us embrace as partners, these.
Now is the time; let it be so.

Such fear comes forth.
I had forgotten what a force you are.
Perhaps I thought
Escape was now a possibility
For you had seemed to tame
In times of our communications.
You were not jesting when you said
"Forget me not OR
I will get you for neglecting me."
Mister Gremlin,
What work it is to keep relating
From a place of openness
To darkness, your domain.
I thought that things were getting easier.

Come evil twin,
Come now to join me;
Power surges through
For wholeness,
Now a possibility
At last
Awaits this second coming
Of a sort.
For some, this liberation
Is a mating, yes,
A partnership within the soul
Of golden goodness
With an equal part of dark,
Dense, blackened fear and hate.
This shadow brings emancipation
From the schism;
At long last wholeness,
Soulness,
Dark and light complete.
If only we had known this sooner.

Section 13

REMORSE AND SURRENDER

Sooner.
Wise are those who do it sooner.
Surrender to The One.
We do this when the day is done,
When deathbed gives no other choice.
So why must "I" not have a voice
About my life while I am young?
Why should I turn it over,
Give control away
By saying, "Take me, Spirit,
Make me what you see
that I could be."
By giving not ourselves to God
When we are young
We get to see, eventually
The errors we make,
So many woes
Which aren't undone
Without the Grace which comes
Replacing our remorse
At having not surrendered
Sooner.

Writing on the subject
talking all about
SURRENDER
is not the same
as doing so
for never is the thinking mind
behind the process
except in moving quite behind
and being the caboose, the last in line
as now in letting go
we choose from quite another
level of our personhood
allowing leadership to come
from others places
spacious ones
much smarter, better than our brains
our "bodysense" the wiser venue
if we ask it, it will listen
and may one day simply
give up!
some day
to be lucky we must pray
along the way
that we may gently step aside
and leap with love and trust
into surrenderland

See what happens
When you surrender
See what happens
When you let go
Moving with the flow
You'll know control has limitations
Costing nearly everything
The need to know, to understand
would better be to stand beneath
stand under, looking up
you fill your cup
with holy flowing
ultimate reality
not knowing, only solely slipping
into sweet surrender
letting life unfold
according to
angelic helpers goals
benevolent, beneficent
abundant, overseeing sensitivities
of Heaven

Only for me,
Only for my eyes this poem
Of pain, remorse
Despair as deep as ocean's depth
And only breath can move me through it.
"Only?"
Only breath, you say
When Breath is Life itself!
Why not be glad
For this safari through life's jungle
Of ordeals and pain and fears that stifle,
Only to begin again
The movement into greater presence.
You have achieved awakening;
This, which you have longed for –
To be so real, authentic, whole,
So why the sadness as you reach your goal?
It is the death of your old "friends",
Those patterns, ways in which you've spent
Your days defending lesser fragments
Of your human self –
For what?
Those smaller selves have sought control;
Ironically a competition of a sort ensued
As you surrendered ever more to Spirit, to your Soul.
Your human parts have feared their death
As all the teachers said they would.
And now emancipation from that trap
Could bring you joy and liberation.
Perhaps it isn't yet as near completion as you think,
This process, path, procedure of evolving.
Still miles to go before I sleep/awaken,
Finding freedom ever full.
You thought you knew but didn't really know
Your cup must empty first, then overflow.

Such grief hangs over me
For years,
Days, months,
The time so precious now
These tears all bottled up
For time not richly spent,
And moments gone unlived,
The life that Heaven sent
Which wasn't truly used
For what I might have done.
Forgive me, Self,
For my procrastination
Around the work of living–
Setting free my being
From strife about my wounds.
What's left now?
Do I hear "Abundance?"
Hear I now Your call?
Life, the banquet, still awaits me;
More embodied moments
Followed by Eternity;
Embracing this, my only choice –
These moments which remain
May brokenness no longer drain
Aliveness from my voice
My words, my loving actions;
Choose each moment,
This I vow, to heed Life's call
And now in consciousness,
Aware, awake, I LIVE them all.

To be stuck
When we know that flow
Is what life holds for us–
This is a form of suffering.
Not intense, this mental sluggishness,
Simply not the rich and lively
Movement of fluidity
Which life offers us in living
When the heart's rich
Giving of ourselves is shared.
Be gone, rigidity.
From stagnant energy we are spared
When mind into the heart's space melts
And only then again can joy of life
Be fully felt.

Mix them up
Those pros and cons
Note the choices
Take the good
And simply *see* the bad
And shake them up, those voices
Now feel the balance
Every moment offers us the chance
To know the compensation
Life brings to us
Release frustration
Of this life imperfect
For though it may not be precisely
What we had wanted
It may be perfect it its balance of
the opposites
We simply choose the lighter course
of action
Move away from darker, denser factions
of this world
And choose with consciousness
The way of those who know and show us,
Shine their light for us to move ahead
Instead of chaos choose the
Path of less confusion
Invite profusion of the spaciousness
Transforming darkness.
Be the spark that chooses.
See it ALL.

Do this
Make now a list
Write down those things you wish
Those needs when met -- release themselves
Finding then more peace
Streamline your clear intention
Simply this
To serve Creation
And simply
Be the Light
Reside as often as you might
Allow yourself to do
Within the higher astral plane
Peace is found there
Wisdom, truth and even joy

Section 14

SPIRITUAL CONNECTION

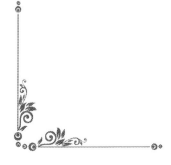

*T*hank God
for quietness
of violet
hues
hanging
'round the silence
which remains
as sounds of chants
subsiding
send believers
deep inside

Sweet baby green ones
Pop like popcorn
Only silently
As Spirit moves
These neonatal
Nubile, clean
Pristine
Clear green
Bright leaves on branches
Springtime brings
Until the Summer sunshine
Blanches them with life's full throttle living
Giving wear and tear to what was innocent
Our hot young living's grand and strong aliveness
Starts to turn the cycle 'round
Then Fall begins to brown and tarnish
What was tender months ago
By dropping those
Which once were popping
So we go below for Winter,
Leaves as compost,
Food for future growth
New gleanings
Greenings
Waiting for renewal
Rebirth
Springtime brings
The jewels
Of baby leaves

Like baby Jesus
Bringing hope
The scope of which cannot be told
But felt within as like a blanket soft
The Holy breathes new life,
Relieving us of grieving
As the Spirit holds us
In its arms
Of new born leaves.

Dear tree,
You spoke to me
I held you and near ecstasy
        Swelled within the marrow of these bones
How could this be
We've only met this afternoon
I'm sure it wasn't in a former life
Your majesty,
        The three of you in one
Your double trunk so friendly
Your strength
I want to play in partnership with you.

An Easter Poem

As the world remembers
Jesus resurrection
(Whatever happened at the time
we'll never know for sure)
I gather now my recollections
of moments when I felt
pathetic, most impure;
of moments when I thought
my life had ended
to only find myself
presented with a door
to yet another chapter
of my life awaiting
to gift me with the new,
of learnings more
from Spirit which adores each seeker,
supporting the unfolding of our lives.
Tomorrow always comes
With rich acceptance;
In our demise we find
A grand surprise.

The following two poems were written at an 8-day Warrior-Monk Retreat in Wisconsin. Our leader, Bill Kauth, directed us to find something in nature to write about. I had seen a tree I loved and made a bee-line for it, but before I got to the tree the SUN tapped me on the shoulder and spoke to me as follows:

Let me warm you, dear one.
Let me fill you with my glowing fire
Like the Sacred Heart
So you again may be that spark
The Sunbeam that you truly are
Bringing hope and joy to many more
Than you have so far
You carry Light for me.
Remember when you feel my rays,
  And see my roundness
I represent your wholeness,
  Fire
  Your heart's desire
To serve my golden beauty
Shining now,
You are my daughter
Speak for me
Show them how
  To hope again
To know their wholeness too
This I'll do in partnership with you.

On this Sun's day
Once long ago
Yet not so long
I came into the world
May twenty second finally called me forth
The Sun became my Light
My warmth
My home
My Leo Moon adores the Sun
Is ruled by its' vibration
Oh Sun, you give me hope anew
You give me power to glow
You want me to be
    With thee
And I shall be a beam,
Beam of Light
Shining here
Below.

When I was two years old, I heard in Sunday School that Jesus loved children and said,

"Let the children come unto me." I learned a song that I sang for years, a song that has resounded in my heart throughout my life: "Jesus wants me for a sunbeam."

Several decades later, early in 1999 I went to the Cenacle in Warrenville, Illinois for a 24 hour solo prayer-retreat to receive guidance and work on my first book. When I arrived there I was hyper with happiness in that wonderful energy field, too jazzed up to imagine being able to write anything. I decided to simply pray to Jesus and ask him to speak to me. I decided to transcribe what I heard, and the following is exactly what I wrote down. The only thoughts that sound like something *I* would say are the words about partnering and balancing opposite energies.

JESUS WANTS YOU FOR A SUNBEAM

Settle down now,
      dear one.
The excitement of your child within
Has you bouncing like a baby
      getting high on joy
Slow down a notch
      so you can hear Me guide you;
You are MY treasure.
Oh, you know that ALL are treasures;
Yet I have a special job for you to do.
Let Me help you focus.
Your mind is so expansive,
      boundless,

joyful,Those mental orgasms
of which you often speak
never cease,
so alive are you
with life.
My joy I give to you,
and as its partner,
peace;
Excitement balanced
with release;
This is a winning duo;
bring them into partnership,
feel them in your heart
knowing well, you do,
this part
is where one's treasures lie
awaiting our awareness
of the riches there within.
Let your mind just spin;
Be a whirling dervish
Like a child
knowing well you do
that trance
and joyful dance
create a space for Me with thee.

You've shown such courage
in your willingness
to look within;

Every form of sin
        you have taken heed of.
Separating self from God,
        sin has been for you
        so painful
-- your wanting Me so much,
-- wanting Me, you do
    the connection that's eluded you.

That connection,
    so hard one,
    is finally, clearly, here for you.

Abuse not now yourself
        by letting others eat you up,
        abuse you, use you.
 What a privilege it is
        to carry Light the way you do,
        to have a mind so bright!
Farewell to the dark night
        your soul has seen so much of.
Tap into it again
        for old time's sake
        from time to time;
But THIS is now your home.
Your residence with Me
        supplies your every need;
        Your life ends happily.

But I have work for you.
This is not the time
for your flight into the Light;
your bodymind must stay
To tell your truths
and play
to love and spread My joy
To every girl and boy you reach.
Go now, my child, to write and teach.

Channeled through Nancy B. Ging 1-25-99

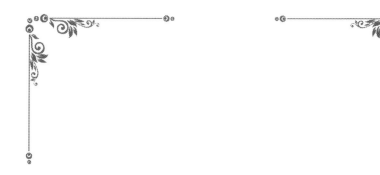

Section 15

A MOTHER'S HEART SPEAKS

a daughter's pain
is only bearable
when mother
moves into surrender
resisting nevermore
to what a life may have
in store for those she's
carried,
heartaches buried
soon will age a mother,
rage will ruin any final stages
of the life remaining for the elder;
only letting go,
resisting not the flow of life
unfolding as it will
becomes the choice
the sensible
and even wondrous
clear response
surrender
simply love anew
receive the happenings,
what 'ere life brings
it's easy for a mother
who may have tried
another way.
resist what happens?
nay
not now,
life brings us to our knees
and what simplicity,
sweet relief it is
to realize the option
can be only One

When a mother
Sees her child
Moving into Selfhood,
Separating from the energetic lineage
Which has been a burden full of agony
Generations of complexity and pain,
These steps forward, onward,
For her children
Upward into higher consciousness
This is joy for a mother
Freedom for the child
Such individuation
Cords unplugged
From infantile attachments,
Stepping into separate Selfhood,
Finding the uniqueness
Honoring the Soul's own choices
Trusting in the Mystery
Dancing with the Light
Brings a sigh of sweet relief
To the one who birthed that babe
Who is now a being –
All one's own.

My son, the mystic
Gifted is he
With shamanic sensibilities,
Groovy healing energies
Attuned so clearly to the Earth
Aligned with trees
With rocks
With critters large and small.
My childhood's Sunday School
Taught that God is Love
And it is so,
Yet there is more I did not know.
Divinity is in the Earth
As well as in our hearts and souls,
My earthy son, the teacher,
Brought me to this knowing
Even as a little boy
Taught me that we're all connected
All things green and growing,
Sharing, bringing messages
To one another
Living creatures one and all.

You light up a room,
>   you do
Your glow,
>   It warms us so.
It's hard to let you go.
You love what's best to love --
Babies, children, Earth --
God knows and loves you so,
>   And you know God
>   And always have;
When you were four you told me so;
Growing then to serve The Force
By showing up
>   in costume, joy and fun,
Your presence sparkling like the sun.
You are my son.
Such pride I harbor in my heart and mind
For one so much
>   in touch with what is right--
Justice, beauty, truth,
>   living in the NOW
Loving so your friends
>   and seeing what is true.
Your sister is an angel too;
And you've seen that,
>   known that,
>   many years.
You've seen beyond her worldly ways,

so practical and good,
seen through to the Soul of her
that surely is pure gold;
So crystal clear with God she is
and you know this;
You see her innocence,
her kindness;
So responsible is she.
She knows not even yet,
how rare a soul she is,
You do, however, know
about HER special glow.
My son, you'll always be alright;
You live secure within the Light.
And now your lives have let me see--
My children have the best of me.

By Kevin Ging
Copyright 1995

About the Author

Nancy Ging received her Psychology degree from Michigan State University. She was inspired in the early 1960's by O. Hobart Mower, the author of *The Crisis in Psychiatry and Religion* and considered getting a M.Div. degree with an intention of integrating spirituality with psychology.

After working one Summer in N.Y.C. as a case aide with heroin addicts at the first Methadone Treatment program in the country Nancy moved on to graduate school. Having been inspired as a teenager by the work of the Rev. Dr. Martin Luther King, Jr., she was blessed to hear him speak twice in Boston. Nancy attended Simmons School of Social Work and, after marrying, worked in the in Washington, D.C. school district. She had two children before the family moved on to the Chicago suburb of Hinsdale, IL. Nancy taught pre-school and Parent Effectiveness Training and studied theology at Bethany School of Theology, Chicago Theological Seminary and the Lutheran School of Theology focusing on the work of Paul Tillich. After receiving her M.S.W. degree from George Williams College she earned a post-graduate certificate in Marriage and Family Therapy from the Family Institute at Northwestern University and took her early hypnotherapy training at University of Chicago.

Prior to launching into her holistic psychotherapy practice in 1981 she worked in medical and psychiatric settings and as a school social worker in the Chicago suburbs. She also spent time in the study and practice of Buddhism, impressed *by Shambhala, The Sacred Path of the Warrior* by Chogyam Trumgpa Rimpoche and more recently participated in body-centered meditation practices with Dr. Reggie Ray. She has enjoyed Hindu chanting and the wise and delightful teachings of Ram Dass. She appreciates Native American drumming and gong meditations. Nancy continues to enjoy her long membership at the Union Church of Hinsdale.

Nancy's passion is helping people find their own wholeness by teaching how to move energy – sometimes through the reading or writing of poetry. She is a full-spectrum clinician, having woven what she has called the "Energy Paradigm" into her work. Every bit as important to her as her academic background is her training and studies of leading edge therapies such as the many modes of Energy Psychology, learning Energy Medicine from Donna Eden and others, EMDR and several body-centered psychotherapies. She has lectured and taught around the country in both professional, and academic institutions and has been interviewed on television on a number of occasions. Nancy has been a columnist, a consultant and authored the book, *Simplifying the Road to Wholeness* (2001).

Nancy is a mother, a grandmother and mentor to many. All her relationships have expanded her awareness and brought her abundant blessings. She has enjoyed amazing travels, particularly her trips to Peru. Creativity which has taken many forms for this writer, has enriched her life.

Appendix i: Noah's Ark Story

The following is a new take on an old story. Nancy's Noah's Ark anew is something I discovered inside my head during a church service in Denver in 1992. The minister was preaching about Noah. Perhaps I could have paid attention, but the energies of my imagination were more compelling; I went within. This is what I found:

Noah was directed, guided by God/Goddess, a.k.a. The Great Mystery, The Great Spirit, The Super Self, to build an ark. Following the Nike Principle – "Just Do It!", he called into service the energies of his assertive, managerial personality "part" to get the job done. Noah had previously had the good sense to surrender to the leadership of the SuperSelf, and Goodness only knows what he had gone through earlier in his life for Noah to have finally made that decision, yielded to the urge to surrender and allow The Spirit to run the show. He had probably spent a fortune on therapy, sessions with his shaman, buying herbs, essential oils, flower essences, etc.

The Ark was constructed and Noah named it "The Self," honoring and reflecting the Super Self. He welcomed on board all the other energies or "parts" of his personality. Their polar opposite parts were included, nobody was exiled; this kept everything in balance. It was years later that Isaac Newton noticed that every action had an equal and opposite reaction, which made polarities, i.e., parts and their opposites, official — indeed, even respectable. Every energy has an equal and opposite, complementary energy; Chinese medicine, ye olde yin/yang perspective, shows us this for sure. (But the Self, our Soul, is Whole; see Quantum Physics about this).

I've heard that Noah prayed for a wife and God sent him a Goddess, Grace. She surely must have been on board as well for her feminine energies were at least 50 percent of the creative project.

The animals (sometimes appearing in our dreams as symbols of our instinctual, emotional energies) were safe within the Ark, "The Self." It contained them, held them all in harmony. Thank Goodness, for soon it rained excessively. Flooding was all around — unparallelled stress. But the Ark warmly embraced and contained Noah and all his personality parts or patterns of energy, and held them together. Nobody even got seasick.

Super Self (God/Goddess) presented a rainbow overhead and said, "NOW HEAR THIS: YOU ARE PROMISE when you REALIZE you have a Self which holds and keeps all of your personality energies cozy and afloat on whatever the high seas of life may bring."

May you trust your Self and thereby enjoy those still waters frequently as you consciously live through each and every moment of your life.

Appendix ii: Parts and Whole, Selves, Circle and Soul

Frequent meditation on the first image in this book can give the reader the embodied experience of wholeness.

In this image of the large circle holding many small circles, the spacious outer circle represents the loving embrace of one's Soul. This spacious Soul contains the small circles or little selves, patterns of the personality. The polarities, pairs of opposite personality energies, meet in the center where the consciousness of the embodied heart is in partnership with the brain's partnered male and female principles. "Heart-Brain Partnering" creates a healthy self which reflects the larger Soul/Spirit/Self.

1992-1999 Nancy S.B. Ging, L.C.S.W.

Appendix iii: A Unified Theory of the Self

A Unified Theory of Self; Part and Whole, Selves and Soul:

The poem with the beginning lines "Two Hemispheres and one heart" and the image following it pertains to the author's "Unified Theory of Self; Parts and Whole, Selves and Soul (1992)."

Our Soul is our wholeness – the spacious, compassionate container which holds and embraces all that we have experienced as well as our potentials. The Soul-Self is known most clearly through one's heart, the place in one's physical body where Heaven and Earth meet and where the lower three chakras meet the upper three chakras.

Our own Soul-Self is a microcosm of The Creator/ God/ Goddess/All That Is, The One, The Super-Conscious, The Universe, the Macrocosm – or what I shall call The Grand Container Which Holds The Holy Whole. (As The Grand Container "has the whole world in His/Her/It's hands," our individual Essence/Spirit/Soul holds with compassionate acceptance all that we personally experience – mentally, physically, emotionally).

Within the Soul-Self there is the psychological self which CAN become cohesive when the many paradoxes, polarities, or complementary pairs of opposite energy patterns of the personality are in balance and/or held with acceptance in our Consciousness, in the awareness of our Soul-Self. Energetically these pairs are as night and day, yin and yang. We may be aware of one side of the polarity while the other side of that polarity may be in the unconscious (designated by dotted lines in the image). The energies of a part or pattern of personality and its opposite are equally intense as in Newtonian physics: any action has an equal and opposite reaction.

Areas of the brain operating from the male principle (linear or "left brain thinking") will experience and interpret reality as separate or concrete PARTICLES or parts. Areas of the brain functioning from the female principle ("right brain") experience and interpret reality as WAVES of energy in motion. When the brain's dual male/female modes are functioning as a conscious partnership, we may more easily experience heart/Soul sovereignty over the often challenging human condition. Whole-hearted alignment with Heaven and Earth is achieved from the body's experience of the heart's compartments or chambers which are yin (trust, compassion, tenderness, etc.) and yang (courage, joy, stout-heartedness, etc.).

The aware, balanced, cohesive personality or psychological self is a health human's reflection of one's Soul-Self. The personality may be fragmented yet the Soul is always whole.

Appendix iv: Index of first lines

Printed in the United States
By Bookmasters